KNOW HOW KNOW WHY

SPACE

Written by Martin Mobberley

Illustrations by Stephen Sweet

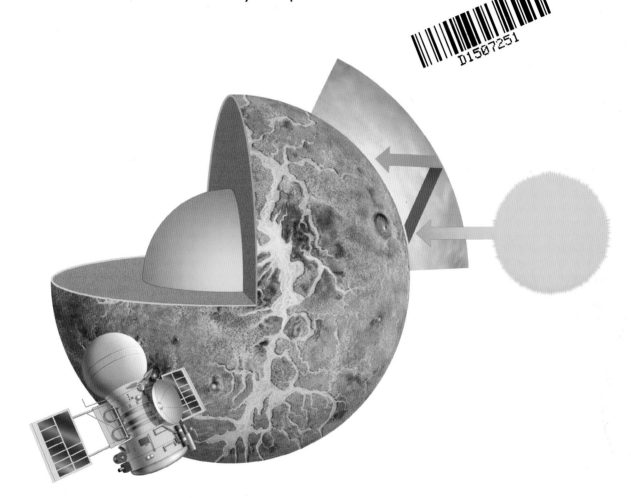

TOP THAT! Kids™

Copyright © 2004 Top That! Publishing plc
Top That! Publishing, 25031 Avenue Stanford,
Suite #60, Valencia, CA 91355
Top That! Kids is a Trademark of
Top That! Publishing plc
www.topthatpublishing.com

THE UNIVERSE

A vast, perhaps infinite, mass of galaxies, older than we can possibly imagine, the universe is measured in "light years" due to its phenomenal size. Whether it was formed by a "big bang," or set to collapse in a "big crunch," scientists have created their own theories about the secrets that it may hold...

How big is the universe ❓

The universe is so big that astronomers use the distance that light travels in one year to measure the parts of it we can see. A beam of light, or a radio wave, travels over 186,000 miles in one second. In just over one second, light can travel from Earth to the Moon. In eight minutes, a beam of sunlight can travel from the Sun to Earth, so the Sun is eight light-minutes away.

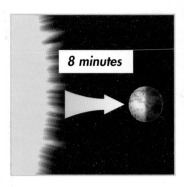

8 minutes

What was the "big bang" ❓

Most astronomers think that around fourteen billion years ago, the universe suddenly came into existence and increased rapidly in size. There was nothing there before the "big bang"—no stars, no galaxies, no space and, wait for it... no time. So there was nothing before the "big bang," because it created time! The universe is still expanding, although the gravitational pull of all the galaxies has slowed the expansion down.

An artist's impression of the "big bang."

How far can astronomers see into the universe ❓

With powerful telescopes, astronomers can see galaxies that are over ten billion light years away. The light from them has taken ten billion years to get to us! More than ten billion light years is almost the same distance as sixty-two billion trillion miles, that's 62,000,000,000,000,000,000,000 miles! That's a very long way! However, we cannot say that the universe definitely "stops" somewhere. We can only judge from what we can see in light years which is galaxies of more than ten billion light years away. We reach a horizon where we can see no more—which means that the universe could go on forever!

A space observatory.

The Hubble space telescope.

The "universe" is the name given to everything out there, and it could be in

FACT BYTES

There are no certain facts to be had about the past and future of the universe.

Different scientists have different explanations for the way things are and do not always agree.

Most believe in a "big bang" theory, others have put forward different theories—what will you believe?

THE SUN

The huge, burning ball of hydrogen that we see rising and setting every day is billions of years old, but is still a hive of activity. On its surface are huge glowing sunspots and solar flares, shooting off heat millions of miles into space, and underneath are golden rays that work their way from the core to reach us.

Where did the Sun come from

The Sun is made up mainly of hydrogen gas, which is the most common element in the universe. When the universe was much younger than it is today, the part of space where our Solar System is now would have been full of hydrogen gas and dust. Over billions of years, this gas and dust would slowly have moved together, due to gravity, and a large amount of hydrogen gas would have concentrated in the middle. As the sheer mass at the center became more concentrated there would have come a point when nuclear reactions began to take place and the gas started to shine! It probably took place about five billion (5,000,000,000) years ago.

Why does the height of the Sun in the sky vary

The height of the Sun in the sky has a huge effect on the temperature. Earth's axis is tilted by just over 23 degrees. If your hemisphere of Earth is tilted towards the Sun (Summer), the Sun will be high up at midday and if your hemisphere is tilted away (Winter) the Sun will be low down. If you live in New York City at 41 degrees North, the Sun can be 72 degrees high in late June at noon, but in late December it will never be higher than 26 degrees above the horizon.

Corona

Convective zone

Radiative zone

Core

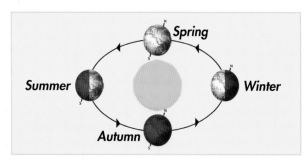

The height of the Sun in the sky depends which way the hemisphere you live in is tilted towards it, meaning that different sides of the world experience opposite seasons at the same time.

WARNING! The Sun is v directly at it and NE

How hot is our Sun ?

The work of Arthur Eddington in the 1930s, and Hans Bethe in the 1950s, came up with answers to this question. Most scientists agree that their theory is the one that fits best. The outside edge of the Sun, known as the corona, gives off light and heat which eventually

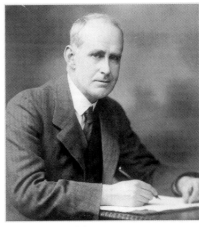

Sir Arthur Eddington.

reaches us. Scientists estimate the temperature here to be around one million degrees Kelvin.

The bit of the Sun that we look at face-on, known as the photosphere, is estimated to be around 5,800°K.

What is a sunspot ?

A sunspot is a darker and cooler region on the Sun's surface caused by intense magnetic activity. The Sun's surface temperature is around 11,000°F, but the center of the sunspot will only be around 7,000°F. The Sun has a diameter more than a hundred times that of Earth, and big sunspots are bigger than Earth too!

FACT BYTES

The corona is the outermost layer of the Sun. It stretches millions of miles into space.

The center of the Sun is made of helium.

The Sun spins around once every 27.4 days.

You should NEVER stare a telescope at it.

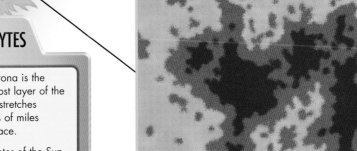

Enlarged area of the Sun depicting a sunspot.

THE SUN

MERCURY

Mercury is the second-smallest planet in our Solar System. It's also the closest to the Sun. With a huge iron core, an extreme range of temperatures, and a very short orbit, astronomers would love to know more about this planet, visited only once by the *Mariner 10* space probe.

How big is Mercury

Mercury has a diameter of 3,032 miles, and is one-third the size of Earth. It is the second smallest of the nine planets in our Solar System.

The respective sizes of Earth (left) and Mercury (right).

How hot is Mercury

Although Mercury is the planet closest to the Sun, Venus is slightly hotter because it has an atmosphere that traps the heat. Mercury has no atmosphere, but the most extreme range of temperatures. They range from 800°F in sunlight to −290°F at night.

800°F

−290°F

Mercury experiences extreme temperature variation.

FACT BYTES

A Mercury year is 88 Earth days long!

Mercury is roughly the same age as the Sun— 4.5 billion years old!

The Mariner 10 space probe.

How many times has it been visited

Only one, unmanned, space probe has been to Mercury. Launched in 1973, *Mariner 10* flew past the planet in 1974 and imaged half of Mercury's surface.

Why does Mercury stay in orbit

Rocky crust

Solid iron core

Mercury is very close to the Sun, but there is no danger of it falling into the Sun. Gravity forces all the planets to rotate "around" the Sun: they would only fall in if they were stopped from going around. As there is no air in space, there is nothing to slow the planets down in their orbits.

How long is Mercury's year

Silicate rock

Mercury orbits the Sun in 88 days, but it rotates on its axis in 59 days. This means Mercury's year is not much longer than its day. This causes the Sun to crawl very slowly across Mercury's sky. However, when Mercury is at its closest to the Sun it gradually speeds up, causing the Sun to stop moving across the sky and move backwards for eight days every year!

When do the orbits of the Sun and Mercury cross

This happens about thirteen or fourteen times each century. The last time was on May 7th, 2003 and the next time will be on November 8th, 2006. Only astronomers with the right equipment can photograph these events,  as the Sun is dangerously bright and will blind anyone who would look at it through a telescope.

The Mercury landscape.

VENUS

Gustav Holst called Venus the "Bringer of Peace" in his famous "Planets" suite. With its bright white clouds, visible in the night sky, it is aptly named. Should we get closer, however, we'd see that under those clouds exists a cratered surface on which nothing could survive, smothered under its boiling hot atmosphere.

An artist's impression of Venus as seen from Earth.

Why is Venus so bright ?

It is partly due to its covering of white clouds, which reflect 75 percent of the Sun's rays back into space. We measure how easy things are to see on a "magnitude" scale. Venus can reach magnitude 4—the brightest object, apart from the Moon, in the night sky.

Has a spacecraft landed on Venus ?

Two Russian spacecraft, *Venera's* 9 and 10, landed on Venus in 1975 and sent back pictures. After an hour they stopped operating, presumably because they melted!

How close is Venus to Earth ?

Venus and Mars both get very near to Earth—relatively speaking! Mars can come within 35 million miles of Earth and did so in August 2003. Venus gets even closer, at 24 million miles from Earth, but is then between us and the Sun so cannot be seen.

Rocky crust

Semi-solid core of iron and nickel

Rocky mantle

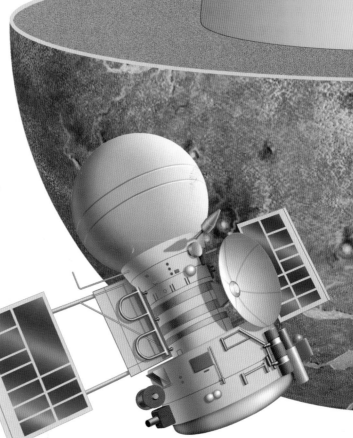

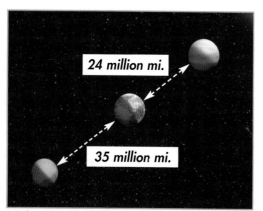

24 million mi.

35 million mi.

Both Mars and Venus get close to Earth.

The Russian Venera 9 that landed on Venus.

...enus' atmosphere

How hot is it on Venus ❓

Venus is three-quarters the distance of Earth from the Sun. If we didn't know better, we might expect it to be a planet where life could exist near the cooler polar regions. However, the surface temperature is a crazy 880°F. This is because the atmosphere is mainly carbon dioxide which makes Venus just like a huge greenhouse, trapping the Sun's heat.

What is Venus' orbit like ❓

Venus sometimes crosses the Sun—twice, close together, and then with a break of over a century! The last time Venus was seen moving in front of the Sun was on December 6th, 1882. It has the most circular orbit of all the planets. It took astronomers a long time to find out the length of Venus' rotation period because thick clouds obscure its surface. Eventually, radar waves were bounced off Venus, allowing them to see the planet clearly.

FACT BYTES

Like Mercury, Venus has a very odd rotation period. It orbits the Sun in 224 days (the Venusian year) but has a "day" of 243 days.

Yes, that's right, the day, is longer than the year!

The surface of Venus could be volcanic.

VENUS

EARTH AND MOON

Our planet is unique, with an atmosphere made of gases existing in perfect harmony to sustain the life underneath. We walk around on the thin crust, suspended on a moving, molten, and plastic-like layer called the mantle. Despite just having one moon, even Earth's tides are affected by its presence.

Why is our Moon so large

Our Moon is relatively large, its diameter being more than a quarter of Earth's.

Our Moon is 2,160 miles in diameter, more than a quarter the diameter of Earth. Only Pluto has a satellite that is larger when compared to itself. There are larger moons in the solar system, but they all belong to the giant planets. Astronomers believe that billions of years ago, another planet passed through the inner Solar System and bumped into Earth, moving lots of molten rock into space. This rock eventually reformed as the Moon.

What shape is Earth ?

A pumpkin shape?

Our planet is not the perfect sphere that you might imagine—it is actually a bit larger around the middle! This makes it slightly pumpkin-shaped. A recent study showed that this bulge was actually on the increase, due to glacial melting at the poles which has led to more water building up around the equatorial area.

What is so special about Earth ?

At about 93 million miles from the Sun, Earth is at exactly the right distance away for things to survive. In addition, Earth's gravity is not too small (it's 7,890 miles in diameter) so the atmosphere doesn't escape, but it's not too big, so lighter, poisonous gases are not retained. Earth also has plenty of water which is essential for life.

Life on Earth's landscape is uniquely sustained.

Why does the Moon appear at different shapes, or phases ❓

The Moon orbits Earth every four weeks, so that there is just over 29 days between full moons. When the Moon is directly behind Earth, the Sun is shining straight onto the side we see, so it looks full. When the Moon is at right angles to the Sun–Earth line it looks half full. When the Moon is close to the Sun in our sky, the other side of the Moon is being illuminated and we just see a crescent. We always see the same side of the Moon though, because it also rotates on its axis in four weeks.

The waning patterns of our Moon.

What is an eclipse ❓

When two things in the sky cross paths, one of the objects will block the light of the other. When the Moon comes between the Sun and Earth, the light reaching us will be affected. This is a "solar" eclipse. If they cross slightly, then we call it a "partial" solar eclipse. If our light is totally blocked, it is known as a "total" eclipse and everything goes dark! You need to be in exactly the right place in the world to experience this. The Sun and the Moon will appear to be the same size and "fit" over each other. When Earth passes between the Sun and the Moon, it is known as a lunar eclipse. The Moon will turn a dark red, as the light passing through our atmosphere is "bent" onto the Moon.

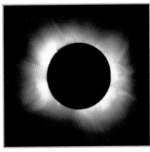

A total eclipse.

FACT BYTES

The amazing combination of gases which make up our atmosphere is 78% nitrogen, 21% oxygen, and 1% of other gases.

Humans haven't existed for very long at all—primitive life began here about 200,000 years ago, but the oldest rocks discovered so far in the Earth's crust are 3,900 million or so years old!

EARTH AND MOON

MARS

Mars has been the focus of science fiction in many movies and novels with reports of strange "Martian canals" on the surface... the "Red Planet" is perhaps the most interesting planet other than Earth, with its series of craters, volcanoes, and canyons, and its two tiny moons.

How long is a "Mars year"

Mars rotates on its axis just like Earth, but it takes a little longer than Earth, which means one Mars day lasts 24 hours and 37 minutes. Mars also goes around the Sun just like Earth, but it takes Mars nearly two Earth years to complete its orbit. This means that a Martian year is 667 days long—nearly twice as long as an Earth year! Mars is about 143 million miles away from the Sun and has a diameter of only 4,220 miles.

Could life exist on Mars

For over 100 years, it was thought that the temperature on Mars, although much colder than on Earth, might sustain life, much as life can exist in the Arctic and Antarctic on Earth. However, when the first space probes flew past Mars in 1965, it showed craters like those on our Moon and measured that the atmosphere was 100 times thinner than Earth's. Nonetheless, Mars probably did have a lot more water and more atmosphere in the past and simple life may once have existed there.

So why do we keep looking ?

Various spacecraft have landed on Mars since the 1970s, but there are no definite signs of life, as yet. However, scientists think simple forms of bacteria might exist under rocks and in water from the polar caps. The latest US mission to Mars landed safely on its surface in January 2004. Its voyage lasted seven months and consisted of over 300 million miles.

Space probes have not found any signs of life on Mars.

Rocky crust

Thousands of asteroids are discovered each year. We know that there are around 30 larger than 120 miles across; many millions are only around 0.6 miles in diameter.

Solid iron core

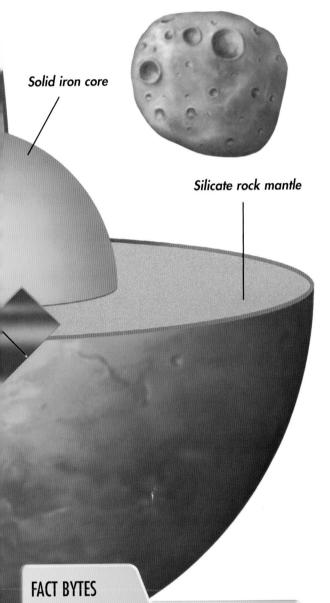

Silicate rock mantle

What is a "captured" asteroid ?

There are hundreds of thousands of asteroids in the asteroid belt between Mars and Jupiter. Mars has two tiny moons, called Phobos and Deimos, which are asteroids that have been "drawn in" or "captured" by Mars' gravity.

What are "Martian canals" ?

In the late 1800s and early 1900s, various astronomers reported seeing straight lines on the Martian surface, when viewed through telescopes. The most famous of these astronomers was the millionaire Percival Lowell, who built a huge telescope in Arizona to study Mars. In an age when people were inspired by voyage and discovery, emphasized by the popularity of Jules Verne's book *Journey to the Center of the Earth,* many people were convinced by his findings. However, by the end of the twentieth century, it was obvious that Mars might only be able to support primitive life—not hardworking canal builders! The canals had been a trick of the eye and the blurring effect of Earth's atmosphere.

FACT BYTES

Mars has a massive volcanic mountain called Olympus Mons, which is over 16 miles high and almost 400 miles across! Its volume is about 100 times larger than Earth's largest volcano.

Mars' surface appears red to us because it contains iron oxide dust. The "blood-like" color is one reason why it is named after the Roman "God of War."

MARS

JUPITER

A true giant, Jupiter has many interesting features, including its famous "Great Red Spot." With incredible gravitational and magnetic fields, it is the largest planet in the Solar System, and the fifth furthest away from the Sun.

How big is Jupiter ❓

Jupiter is huge. It has an equatorial diameter of 88,200 miles, that's eleven times wider than the Earth. In fact, you could fit 1,300 Earths inside Jupiter with room to spare. Despite Jupiter's size, it spins on its axis in just under ten hours.

How far is Jupiter from the sun ❓

Jupiter is about 480 million miles from the Sun—around five times further away than Earth. Light, traveling at 186,000 miles per second, takes over 40 minutes to get to Jupiter. As it is so far away, it takes nearly twelve Earth years to orbit the Sun. The distance between Jupiter and its nearest neighbor, Saturn, is also massive. Saturn is twice as far from Earth as Jupiter is! There are 387 million miles between them.

93 million mi.

Jupiter   Earth

480 million mi.

Why has it got so many moons ❓

Jupiter has over twenty moons, and more small moons are being discovered every year. It has so many because it is so massive and over billions of years has captured more and more objects in its huge gravitational field. The largest moons, called Io, Europa, Ganymede, and Callisto, are similar in size to our own Moon. These four moons can be spotted as faint stars through a small pair of binoculars. Jupiter's gravity pulled the comet Shoemaker-Levy 9 into the giant planet in July 1994. Jupiter was covered in "bruises" from the impact for months afterward.

Atmosphere

Outer mantle

Inner mantle

Rocky core

Europa
Diameter 1,950 miles

How strong is Jupiter's magnetism ?

Jupiter has the strongest magnetic field of any planet in the Solar System. The field is 40 times stronger than that of Earth and is generated, deep within Jupiter by electric currents in a strange liquid called metallic hydrogen, deep within Jupiter. This also gives rise to powerful radio emissions.

Why can't we land on Jupiter ?

Jupiter does not have a surface as such. The features we see are all part of its upper atmosphere. If you sent a spacecraft to Jupiter, it would just descend through more and more dense layers of hydrogen gas, which eventually become metallic hydrogen liquid. Somewhere, very deep inside there is probably a rocky core.

What is the Great Red Spot ?

The Great Red Spot is a gigantic rotating storm, bigger than the whole of Earth, which is found in Jupiter's southern hemisphere. The storm is so large that it has survived for at least 170 years and maybe for over 300 years. It can easily be seen using a small telescope.

— **Great Red Spot**

Callisto
Diameter 2,986 miles

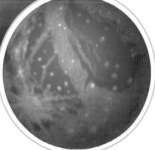

Ganymede
Diameter 3,272 miles

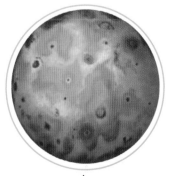

Io
Diameter 2,256 miles

SATURN

With its massive spinning ring system, partly held in their orbits by the gravitational pull of tiny moons, Saturn is one of the most beautiful objects in our night sky. The planet itself is nearly all gas—probably with a rocky core. A little smaller than Jupiter, this planet is the second largest in our Solar System.

Why has Saturn got rings ?

Did an icy moon break up to form Saturn's rings?

Many astronomers think that Saturn's rings may be the result of an icy moon, maybe 190 miles across, that came too close to Saturn and broke up. Saturn is not the only planet to have a system of rings. The other giant planets, Jupiter, Uranus, and Neptune, have extremely feeble ring systems, which are too faint to be seen from Earth. Saturn's spectacular rings make it the most beautiful object to see through a telescope.

The outer mantle is around 12,000 miles thick, and made from hydrogen molecules.

This layer is comprised mainly of metallic hydrogen.

Saturn has a rocky core, perhaps 9,000 miles across.

How thick are the rings ?

Approximately every fifteen years, Saturn's rings are "edge on" to Earth. Although the rings span a distance of over 167,000 miles, they are made up of millions of icy chunks, probably less than 30 feet across (although some are house-sized!) When the rings reach this position, they are less than 600 feet thick and virtually disappear.

The rings are made from icy chunks such as this.

FACT BYTES

Saturn spins so fast that centrifugal force causes the equator to bulge outwards—it looks a little like a squashed basketball!

Astronomers have discovered daytime clouds on Titan and believe it may have an atmosphere—which means it might be able to support life.

Jupiter has a diameter of 88,850 miles

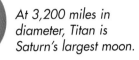

At 3,200 miles in diameter, Titan is Saturn's largest moon.

atmosphere is ~ved to be about ~ miles deep.

What is Saturn's largest moon

Although Saturn has no moons as easy to see as Jupiter's four big moons, it does have a moon called Titan, which is over 3,000 miles in diameter. It orbits Saturn around once every sixteen days. It is easy to spot with a big pair of binoculars or a telescope.

Why is there a big gap between the rings

Astronomers knew little about the gaps in the rings before space probes visited the planet. The largest of these gaps is called the Cassini division and is nearly 3,000 miles wide. The gaps are formed by the gravitational pull of Saturn's moons on the millions of icy chunks making up the rings. The gravitational force of the moon Mimas causes the Cassini gap.

Can I see the rings with a telescope

If a telescope is on a tripod and Saturn's rings are wide open, a magnification of less than twenty times will reveal the rings, but 100 times will show them very clearly. To the naked eye Saturn looks just like a bright star.

How large is Saturn

Saturn has an equatorial diameter of over 75,000 miles, so it is a bit smaller than Jupiter. However, the visible rings span 167,000 miles from tip to tip, which is nearly twice the diameter of Jupiter. Unfortunately, Saturn is a very long way from the Sun—over 895 million miles. This is almost twice as far as Jupiter and so it appears much smaller. As it is so far away, it takes over 29 years to orbit the Sun.

has a ~eter of ~0 miles

URANUS

With its beautiful blue-green appearance, Uranus must have been an exciting discovery for astronomers. Among its distinctive features are a strange rotation system and many moons, all of which are named after characters found in the writings of Alexander Pope and William Shakespeare. It has a narrow ring system, but unlike those of Saturn which are pale in color, they are dark, being made from dark-colored dust particles.

How was Uranus discovered

Herschel discovered Uranus from his yard!

Uranus was discovered on March 13th, 1781 by William Herschel, using a hand-made telescope from the back yard of his house in Bath, England. The house has now been made into a museum. Herschel thought Uranus was a comet when he first saw it. In 1787, he discovered two of Uranus' moons—Titania and Oberon.

You couldn't breathe on Uranus, as methane makes the atmosphere poisonous.

What is the strangest thing about Uranus

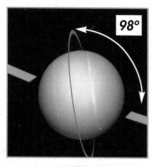

Its axis of rotation is tilted by 98 degrees, so it rotates on its side, every seventeen hours. No other planet does this, although Venus, rotating slowly backwards, is just as weird! Astronomers believe some kind of collision, billions of years ago may have caused Uranus' 98 degree tilt. Astronomers expect everything in the solar system to rotate in the same direction as the Sun and the orbits of the planets: Uranus does not do this and it is a real mystery as to the reason why!

Uranus' tilt means it also has a strong magnetic field, 60 degrees to the rotation axis.

Ariel
er 721 miles

Umbriel
Diameter 1,000 miles

Mantle with ammonia,
methane and icy,
gaseous water

Rocky core

Atmosphere of
hydrogen, helium,
and methane

Titania
Diameter 982 miles

Oberon
Diameter 963 miles

How many moons are there ?

Uranus has over twenty moons, with five big ones. The big ones are called Miranda, Ariel, Umbriel, Titania and Oberon. Miranda is less than 310 miles in diameter. The other four range from 721 to 1,000 miles. Miranda has a strangely grooved and cratered surface and is unlike any other moon in the solar system.

With its carved surface, Miranda is unique. It could have been shattered by another moon crashing into it, reforming with a crazy jagged surface.

How can Uranus be spotted ?

In theory, Uranus can be seen as a faint star with the naked eye from a very dark site, 75 miles from the nearest big city. You need a pair of binoculars or a small telescope to see it easily. With a large telescope, it appears as a greenish disc. It can be seen all year round in the constellation of Aquarius and is best seen in August.

How far away is the Sun ?

Uranus is about 1,800 million miles from the Sun. That's twice as far away as Saturn! Light from the Sun takes nearly three hours to reach Uranus. At over 30,000 miles in diameter, Uranus is a giant planet, but it is still less than half the diameter of Saturn.

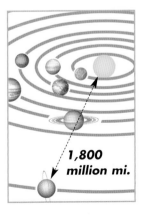

1,800 million mi.

FACT BYTES

Uranus is the third largest planet in the Solar System.

The reason Uranus is blue-green is because the methane gas in the atmosphere absorbs red light.

NEPTUNE

In 1989, the *Voyager 2* space probe flew past Neptune, the outermost of all the gas giants. The race to discover Neptune had been on many years before, and was finally won in 1846. A huge distance away from the Sun, this planet has an incredibly cold atmosphere and an icy mantle. It also has eight moons, one of which moves very strangely!

Atmosphere of hydrogen, he and methane

How was Neptune hunted down ?

Neptune was the first planet that astronomers actually hunted down. Mercury, Venus, Mars, Jupiter, and Saturn are all visible to the naked eye and have been for many years. Neptune was discovered by Galle and D'Arrest at Berlin Observatory, in 1846. D'Arrest suggested they use the latest star chart which had only just been produced. It took them less than 30 minutes to locate a star not on their map. However, they were not the first to guess that there was an "eighth planet."

Mantle of ice, methane, and ammonia

Galle and D'Arrest put Neptune on the map.

How far away is Neptune ?

Rocky silicate core

Neptune orbits the Sun at a distance of 2,800 million miles. It is thirty times further from the Sun than Earth is and it takes 165 years to complete an orbit. At this distance from the Sun, it is very cold. The temperature at Neptune's equator is about −380°F.

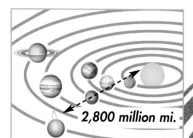

2,800 million mi.

FACT BYTES

Neptune has three main rings, which vary in thickness. This was confirmed by the *Voyager 2* space probe.

Neptune's color reminds us of the sea—
and it is thought to have an ocean of
liquid methane and ice slush. Nice!

*Is Triton a captured
object from a distant
part of the Solar System?*

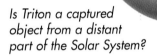

What is Triton ?

Triton, which is 1,680 miles across, orbits the
planet backwards every six days! Weird!
Astronomers think that Triton must have been a stray
object from a distant part of the solar system that was
captured as it moved near Neptune. When the
spacecraft *Voyager 2* flew past Triton in 1989, it found the
moon to be smaller and brighter than expected with a large,
slightly pink, polar cap at the south. The surface of Triton is at a
freezing −390°F and there are nitrogen ice fountains that shoot
nitrogen ice and dark dust particles several miles into the air!

What does Neptune look like ?

Neptune and Uranus are almost identical in many
ways, being about 30,000 miles in diameter and
colored blue-green. Neptune rotates every sixteen
hours, and Uranus, seventeen. However, astronomers
believe Neptune's core is hot, while Uranus' is cold.

Neptune (left) looks similar to Uranus (right).

NEPTUNE

PLUTO

A tiny planet and the furthest away in our Solar System, Pluto is named after the god of the underworld. Its moon, Charon, is around half the size of Pluto itself. The diameter of this rocky, icy planet is 1,430 miles. Astronomers believe that Pluto could be visited, with a little help from Jupiter's gravity, which would "slingshot" a rocket all the extra way to the edge of the Solar System.

Crus

Core of rock and ice

Icy mantle

Who discovered Pluto, and how did they do it ?

Pluto was discovered by Clyde Tombaugh in 1930. He was a young farm worker, employed to work at the Lowell Observatory in Arizona because of his skill in observing the planets through his home made telescope. He discovered Pluto while checking photographic plates in a deliberate search. Calculations by astronomers indicated that there might be a ninth planet near where Tombaugh was searching. However, after its discovery, it was found to be too small to be the planet they were looking for!

Clyde Tombaugh.

Is Pluto a real planet ?

As recently as 1999, the International Astronomical Union debated whether Pluto should be renamed as asteroid number 10,000. The problem is that Pluto is only 1,430 miles in diameter. This means that there are eight moons of Jupiter, Saturn, Neptune, and Earth that are larger than Pluto! However, the first planet, Mercury, is also smaller than Jupiter's moon Ganymede and Saturn's moon Titan. In the end, astronomers decided to keep Pluto as a planet. It is, after all, larger than any of the asteroids.

What astronomers believe Pluto's surface might be like.

How far is Pluto from the Sun ?

Pluto has a highly elliptical orbit which takes it as far as 4,600 million miles from the Sun and as close as 2,700 million miles. One orbit takes 248 years to complete! At its closest, it can be closer to the Sun than Neptune and this actually happened between 1979 and 1999. Light takes between four and seven hours to travel from the Sun to distant Pluto. No spacecraft has ever been to Pluto.

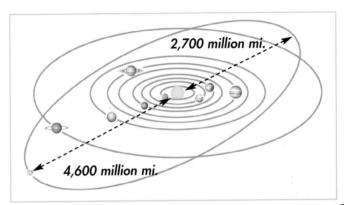

2,700 million mi.

4,600 million mi.

What is Charon ?

Charon was discovered in 1978, when astronomer James Flagstaff noticed that images of Pluto were slightly elongated on photographs he had taken. Charon and Pluto are so close together that they can be regarded as a double planet. Charon is 790 miles in diameter, slightly more than half the diameter of Pluto. The two are separated by only 12,200 miles and they orbit each other in the same time it takes Pluto to rotate, that is, in six days and nine hours. So Pluto and Charon are a bit like two ends of a dumbbell, with one end half as big as the other!

Charon is half the size of Pluto. The planet and its moon are very close to each other—only 12,200 miles apart.

as very keen to
was not found until
in 1930.

e size of our Moon!

THE STARS

When you look up into the night sky and see it filled with stars, just think that each one could be like our own sun, capable of supporting life and its own Solar System. Of all different ages and sizes, stars continue to be born, and to die. We tend to view them in groups called constellations, which help us to make sense of the sheer size and distance of stars themselves.

Where's the nearest star ?

The closest star is just over four light years away, and the dimmest stars we can see without a telescope are thousands of light years away. We see nearby stars as they looked several years ago and faraway stars as they looked thousands of years ago.

With the naked eye, we can see stars four light years away.

Why are stars different colors ?

It all depends on the temperature of the star. Our Sun is a yellowish color because it has a surface temperature of just under 11,000°F. A star like Betelgeuse in Orion looks red because it is cooler, around 5,500°F. The blue star Rigel, also in Orion, is much hotter, over 18,000°F. Blue stars are hotter than our Sun; red stars are cooler.

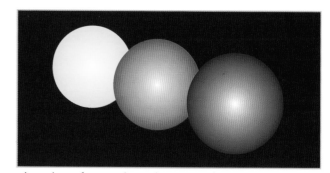

The colors of a star depends on its surface temperature.

What are the "hemispheres' ?

Earth is split around the middle by an imaginary line called the equator. Whether you are situated above or below it determines whether you're in the northern or southern hemisphere. The stars you can see depends on your position. The most easily recognizable star in the northern hemisphere is the Pole Star (Polaris). The southern hemisphere's most famous star is the Dog Star (Sirius).

Spot some famous star constellations in the northern hemisphere: 1) Pegasus, 2) Cygnus, 3) Cassiopeia, 4) Bootes, 5) Ursa Major, 6) Leo, 7) top of Orion.

In the southern hemisphere, you can see: 1) bottom of Orion,
2) Canis Major, 3) Phoenix, 4) Southern Cross, 5) Pavo, 6) Scorpius.

What is a constellation ?

A constellation is simply a set of stars that have been put into a group, and given a name. There are 88 groups of stars that can be called constellations. Many of them were named by the Ancient Greeks, such as Ptolemy, after animals and people from myth and legend.

FACT BYTES

The Sun you felt on your skin today was produced one million years ago! It takes an immense amount of time for the rays to work their way to the solar surface.

What is a "nova' ?

A "nova," meaning "new star," can appear when a binary star system has an outburst, making it 100,000 times brighter than normal. The outburst is caused by hydrogen gas falling onto another, denser, star. This causes a nuclear explosion on the denser star's surface. There are also "supernova" events where a star comes to the end of its life, but these are very rare. Astronomers have not seen a bright supernova in our galaxy for over 400 years.

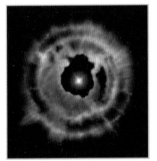

A nova is 100,000 brighter.

A star reaches the end of its life.

How long do stars last ?

It all depends how much hydrogen the star started off with. Heavy stars tend to burn brightly but die out quickly. Don't worry! Our Sun has billions of years of useful life left before it runs out of hydrogen. It is around half-way through its "life" as a star.

Our star will burn for much longer before running out!

GALAXIES

Vast, rotating masses of stars, held together by gravitational attraction, galaxies exist in huge numbers. Our Solar System forms part of the galaxy known as the Milky Way which consists of maybe 100 to 200 billion other stars and measures around 100,000 light years across!

How big is our galaxy ?

A galaxy is simply a vast collection of stars that form some kind of recognizable shape. Our galaxy probably contains well over one hundred thousand million stars (100,000,000,000). Astronomers think it is nearly 100,000 light years across, but only 2,000 light years thick. By comparison, our Solar System is less than about one light day across. So the galaxy is over 36 million times wider! To make sense of such large figures, imagine a plate around 6 feet across. About 1 foot from the edge is our Solar System. Most of the stars around the edge of the "plate" are the new ones. The great bulge in the center of our galaxy is known as the nucleus, and contains old stars.

Where is our Solar System located inside our galaxy ?

We are nearer to the edge than the middle. When we look into the night sky and see the Milky Way we are seeing through the edge of our galaxy. When we look at the southern constellations of Sagittarius and Scorpius, we are looking towards the central bulge of the galaxy, but when we look towards constellations like the W-shaped Cassiopeia, we are looking out through the disc of our galaxy.

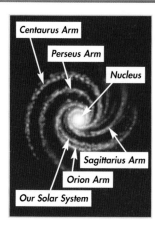

Centaurus Arm
Perseus Arm
Nucleus
Sagittarius Arm
Orion Arm
Our Solar System

Our galaxy edge-on.

FA

What is Andromeda

The Andromeda galaxy, also known as Messier 31 (or M31), is only two million light years away and, from dark country sites, can be seen as a faint smudge of light. In the southern hemisphere, the large and small Magellanic clouds can be seen too. They are small companion galaxies orbiting our own galaxy.

How many galaxies are there

Billions! Astronomers can see countless galaxies as they look farther back in space and time with huge telescopes and with the Hubble space telescope.

This image from the Hubble space telescope shows galaxies outside our own.

An example of a spiral galaxy.

What shapes are galaxies

There are three types of shape. Spirals, shaped like pinwheels, look like our own galaxy, the Milky Way. Irregular galaxies have no definite shape at all. Elliptical galaxies are oval-shaped. They are more likely to be the oldest type as, running out of fresh gas, they cannot create many new stars and form a fixed shape. Irregular and spiral galaxies are still growing and their shapes will change as new stars are born.

it takes 225 million years for
Since it formed, some eleven
as rotated about fifty times.

astronomers believe that there
llion stars in our galaxy and
0 to 120 billion galaxies in the
see.

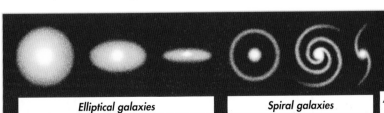

| Elliptical galaxies | Spiral galaxies | An irregular galaxy |

BLACK HOLES

Black holes form much of the material for science fiction writers and movie makers. The idea that a star could collapse, leaving behind a hole with a mind-bogglingly strong gravitational pull, is one of the main theories to account for strange X-rays emitting from space. Their existence has not been proved—but they are a highly exciting idea.

What is a black hole **?**

A black hole is a region of space where gravity is so powerful that not even light can escape—this is why the hole is "black." The speed an object must move at in order to escape from a star or planet's gravity is called "escape velocity." To escape from Earth's gravity, you have to travel at 25,000 mph. The Sun has an escape velocity of over 1.2 million miles per hour. A black hole has an escape velocity faster than the speed of light, so if light can't escape from a black hole, nothing can! The edge of a black hole is known as the "event horizon"—the point of no return. Even if something could get inside a black hole, there would be no way that it could "report back" as it would disappear completely, and forever!

How do we know they exist **?**

Serious work on black holes started in the 1960s, but no-one can say for sure whether they actually exist. The strongest evidence seems to be the strange "X-rays" that satellites pick up when orbiting Earth. We cannot see them so it is only their weird gravitational pull that suggests their existence.

How does a black hole form **?**

The most likely cause of a black hole, or so astronomers think, is a massive star coming to the end of its life. The star collapses, because the fuel has run out, and the energy provided by the nuclear reactions can no longer support the star's weight. When the star collapses it becomes very dense and its gravitational pull increases. If the escape velocity exceeds the speed of light, the star is swallowed by its own gravity and only the gravitational pull remains.

FACT BYTES

A feather would weigh several billion tons in a black hole!

If an astronaut "fell" into a black hole, he or she would be stretched like a piece of spaghetti by the huge gravitational pull.

The star collapses after all of its "fuel" runs out.

The star becomes very dense.

The star is swallowed by its own gravity.

Is there another universe ?

Think of a black hole, everything sucked inside it, meeting a black hole running the other way up (a white hole). Now imagine the point at which they meet—a passage called a wormhole. This could connect one universe to another... An exciting idea, it is just a theory which defies scientific "rules."

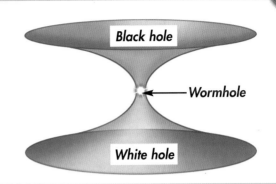

Black hole

Wormhole

White hole

Event horizon

Black hole

Spiraling hot gases

ck hole
sit in the
of our galaxy!

How massive are black holes ?

Weight and mass are not the same thing. Weight depends on where the object is (on Earth, for example), but mass measures the amount of material there is. When we talk about how massive black holes are, we mean how much stuff they contain. The black holes at the center of galaxies were probably each as massive as one star when they first formed, but have sucked in a million or more over time!

CELESTIAL BODIES

It's all happening up there... comets, meteors, and asteroids, whizzing around the Sun, producing amazing shows of light. Members of NASA have devised a mechanism called the Torino Scale to assess the damage celestial bodies could do if they hit Earth. Fortunately, any serious collisions with the Earth are incredibly rare—the Manicouagan crater in Quebec, Canada has a rim diameter of 60 miles, but is believed to have been formed around 212 million years ago!

What is a comet ?

A typical comet is a chunk of icy and rocky material that is between 0.6-30 miles in diameter. If this icy chunk gets close to the Sun, it heats up and the icy material evaporates, creating the comet's head. The radiation from the Sun then blows some of the material away from the head, creating a tail. The comet's tail can be millions of miles long even though the comet itself is small.

An icy comet...

...heats up via the Sun.

What is a meteor? Is it the same sort of thing ?

A meteor is a tiny particle which enters Earth's atmosphere from space. Typically, it might only be the size of a grain of sand but, as it heats up and glows, it looks like a star shooting across the sky. Some meteors are much bigger though and, occasionally, a bright meteor is too big to burn up and may leave a small stone on the ground. However, finding them is almost impossible! The Perseid meteor shower (around August 12th) and the Geminid meteor shower (around December 13th) enable more meteors to be seen than normal, but it's best to look after midnight.

A "shooting star."

How many are out there ?

The LINEAR and NEAT telescopes in the USA have discovered hundreds of thousands of tiny asteroids, mainly between Mars and Jupiter. Astronomers also know of over 1,000 comets, although most are too faint to be seen without a big telescope. The possibility of an asteroid hitting Earth is measured on the Torino Scale. However, astronomers have calculated that the chance of a collision with Earth large enough to cause major damage averages out at once every 300,000 years!

BYTES

...ets' tails don't point ...e direction they're ...ing, but are ...ed away from the ...y solar winds.

... is some evidence ...William the ...queror saw Halley's ...t in 1066.

Can I see a comet ?

Really bright comets from deep space, like Hyakutake in 1996 and Hale-Bopp in 1997, are only discovered a year or two before they become bright. Every few years, a comet becomes visible to the naked eye, and with binoculars, or a small telescope, you can see comets every year.

Some comets are visible to the naked eye.

What is the difference between an asteroid and a comet ?

The main difference between asteroids and comets is what they're made of. While comets are made up of dust, ice, and rocky material, asteroids are formed from rocky material and some metals. This means that asteroids don't have a tail, as no ice evaporates from them. Asteroids orbit the Sun, mainly between the planets Mars and Jupiter. They range in size from 0.6-60 miles across. The four largest asteroids known to astronomers are named Ceres, Pallas, Juno, and Vesta.

Heat creates the comet's impressive tail which can be millions of miles long.

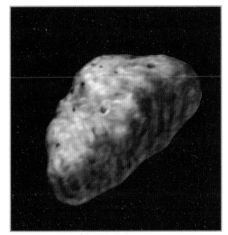

Asteroids reach 100 miles across.

The bright spot is called the nucleus.

CELESTIAL BODIES

EARLY ROCKETS

Without the rocket, we'd know very little about the things you are reading about in this book. We might be able to see certain planets, and our Moon, but we'd never be able to visit them. Space rockets have developed from those used in war and their technologies regarding propulsion (the force needed for lift-off) are similar—read about the pioneers of rocket technology here.

Who invented the rocket

The first rockets may have been invented as early as the tenth century, by the Chinese, but they were little more than flying "fire-arrows" filled with flammable material. By the thirteenth century, however, primitive fireworks and rockets filled with gunpowder were in regular use. In the early 1800s, a military man Colonel William Congreve, based at Woolwich Arsenal, England, developed a range of rocket missiles which could be launched from special ships in battle.

Congreve—"The rockets red glare."

Congreve rockets were built on long poles to make them easy to carry into battle.

The first liquid fuel rocket.

What was a liquid fuel rocket ?

The American Robert Goddard launched the first liquid fuel rocket on March 16th, 1926. It used liquid oxygen and gasoline as the propellant. The rocket was over 10 feet long and reached a height of almost 200 feet and a speed of over 60 mph. By 1935, his best rocket was nearly 16 feet long and could climb to a height of over 1.2 miles at a speed of over 600 mph.

Dr. Robert Goddard with an early liquid fuel rocket.

Who was the first man to design a space rocket

The Russian Konstantin Tsiolkowsky (1857-1935) designed the first space rockets although he never actually built any. He was simply a mathematician and physicist who realized that liquid oxygen and liquid hydrogen would provide the best rocket fuel. His theory, the "Tsiolkovsky Formula," analyszed the relationships between rocket speed and gas pressure. It was 100 years before the *Sputnik 1* was launched by the Russians.

Konstantin Tsiolkowsky.

The V2 rocket was an impressive development and stood over 50 feet tall. Launched from the Netherlands, it could fly to London in five minutes at speeds of over 3,000 mph.

Who was Wernher von Braun

Wernher von Braun was one of the most important pioneers of rocket development. He was employed under the Nazi regime to build their V1 and V2 rockets and later transferred to NASA to help develop the *Saturn* rockets. He was the chief architect of the *Saturn V* launch vehicle, and is ultimately responsible for getting the first people to the Moon. This technology has been used in many lunar landings since—(see pages 38-39).

FACT BYTES

NASA stands for National Aeronautics and Space Administration.

It was set up in 1958 as a worldwide body for space exploration and discovery.

The V1 rocket, designed by Wernher von Braun.

Who launched the first satellite into orbit ❓

Despite the United States of America employing Wernher von Braun, it was the Russians who put the first satellite into orbit. This was *Sputnik 1*, launched on October 4th, 1957. To do this required the final stage of the rocket to reach a speed of over 17,000 mph! The Russians achieved this success because their nuclear bombs were so heavy that they had developed incredibly powerful rocket engines many years before the Americans.

The Sputnik 1 *satellite.*

MANNED ROCKETS

Once rocket technology had been developed, it was soon realized that, if a missile could be sent across the world to bomb another country, rockets could be sent up into space. For over ten years, the Soviet Union and America were locked in a development battle known as the "Space Race." In 1957, the Soviet Union launched the first artificial satellite, *Sputnik 1,* and America landed a man on the Moon in 1969.

How fast do rockets go

Before landing on Earth, rockets can travel up to 25,000 mph. As they re-enter Earth's atmosphere and prepare for touchdown, the speed drops to a few hundred mph. Once the parachute has been released, they slow to a safe speed before landing, on land or in the water—if all goes to plan!

Spacecraft landing safely in the ocean with a parachute.

What was the first moon rocket

The first manned spacecraft to go around the Moon and come back to Earth was *Apollo 8* in December 1968. *Apollo 9* tested the Lunar Module out, but only in Earth's orbit. *Apollo 10* went to the Moon and descended to within 6 miles of the lunar surface, and then *Apollo 11* landed in the Moon's "Sea of Tranquility" on July 20th, 1969.

Why are rockets so huge ?

At the beginning of the race to send a rocket to the Moon, there was no single rocket powerful enough to force through Earth's gravity. The answer to this problem came in the form of rocket stages—putting smaller rockets into giant multi-stage launch vehicles that would tackle each part of lift-off with different sections containing fuel supplies to aid the engines. After each rocket "stage" has used up its fuel, the stages are thrown away, keeping the rocket as light as possible.

Who was the first man in space ?

The Cosmonaut, Yuri Gagarin, was the first man into space and to orbit Earth. His spacecraft, *Vostok 1,* was launched on April 12th, 1961. Less than a month later, the US Space Administration NASA launched their first astronaut, Alan Shepard, into space, but he did not orbit Earth and his Mercury-Redstone rocket only reached a speed of 8,300 mph. In July 1961, NASA launched Edward Grissom into space, too. Finally, on February 20th, 1962, NASA launched John Glenn to orbit Earth in his Mercury spacecraft *Friendship 7.*

Cosmonaut, Yuri Gagarin.

Astronaut, Alan Shepard.

Payload

gen tank

Fuel tank

ird-stage engine

gen tank

Fuel tank

ond-stage engine

gen tank

Fuel tank

irst-stage engines

This diagram is a simplified version of the three-stage Saturn V moon rocket.

Third stage

The third stage is boosted into orbit with a smaller engine, which is discarded with stages one and two once the spacecraft is safely in orbit, or on the way to the Moon.

Second stage

Liquid oxygen in the oxygen tank mixes with the fuel in the fuel tank of the second-stage engine, pushing the rocket to a higher altitude— around 115 miles.

First stage

The first-stage rocket contains enough fuel to feed the engines which provide enough lift for the huge weight of the rocket to escape gravity (i.e.—not fall back down again!).

The *Ariane 5,* launched on October 21st, 1998, marked the beginning of a new style of heavyweight rocket. Its total height (including all stages) is from 147-183 feet tall, with a diameter of 40 feet. The *Saturn V* rocket that launched the Apollo spacecraft weighed over 3,000 tons, and nearly all of that weight was fuel!

Most of this rocket contains fuel for the mission.

MANNED ROCKETS

INSIDE A SPACECRAFT

Living in space may seem like fun! After all, there's no gravity to hold you down, and all that floating around must be a real laugh. However, simple things we take for granted here on Earth, like taking a shower and going to the toilet, are a mission of their own inside a spacecraft. All astronauts must go through lots of preparation before they are considered ready for a journey that could last for months.

The Shuttle is divided into three sections: the flight deck, living quarters, and lower deck. Everything, including the astronauts when they go to bed, must be strapped down!

What happens to the astronaut **?**

The body's weightlessness in space means that the bone and muscles can easily waste away as they have little work to do in hauling a heavy body about. In addition, without gravity the spine starts to relax, and astronauts can easily be 2 inches taller at the end of a mission. This height increase quickly goes away again after a few days back on Earth. To keep fit the astronauts eat a special diet and exercise regularly while they are weightless. More than two-thirds of astronauts suffer from motion sickness, although most recover after a few days in space.

Controls for

Observation window

Pilot's seat

Bunk beds

Exercise

Astronauts can become taller in space as lack of gravity causes the spine to relax.

Why are spacesuits essential **?**

There is no air in space, so there is nothing to breathe. A spacesuit provides astronauts with air. Also, because there is no air, there is no air pressure. Even if an astronaut could hold his breath he could not go into the vacuum of space as his lungs would burst from the pressure inside his body. Spacesuits provide protection from the extreme temperatures in space too. Cold water was pumped around the suits used on the Moon to keep the astronauts cool. The helmet on a spacesuit provides a protective dark visor to reduce the intense sunlight in space.

How do astronauts take a shower ?

Water is a very precious resource in space, so astronauts can go for days without a shower, just sponging themselves with damp cloths. On some spacecraft, a special "shower" unit is fitted. The astronaut gets into the cylinder, shuts the door, and then soaps up with a wet pad—lack of gravity means that the water sticks to the body, so it has to be rubbed off. Any soapy mess is sucked up using a special attachment!

Conmmander's seat

A space shower is very different than on Earth!

How do astronauts eat food in space ?

In space, everything is weightless, which makes eating a normal meal impossible. All the food and the knives, forks, and plates would just float around! Liquids would float away from cups, too. So the astronauts have special plastic packs of food containing big packets of sauce which they can suck through a straw. Some of the meals are dehydrated so they add water to them through a straw, and then suck them up. Surprisingly, food swallowed in space does end up in the astronauts' stomachs, as the act of swallowing still forces food and drink in the right direction!

ilet area

Eating area

Ladder to flight deck

Space food must be freeze-dried.

FACT BYTES

There are no definite explanations as to why food tastes different in space. Some astronauts pack plenty of their favorite food, only to find they can't stand it after liftoff!

Astronauts often suffer from "stuffy head"—they feel "blocked up" around the upper half of the body because their blood flows in an upward direction!

Food must be freeze-dried to remove water to make it as light as possible. Bizarrely, the nutritional value remains nearly the same!

Grub's up!

MOON LANDING MISSIONS

The world watched with bated breath as NASA landed men on the Moon in 1969. From 1969 to 1972, six missions and twelve astronauts landed on the Moon, but there have been no more landings for over 30 years. The Chinese may have plans to put a person on the Moon, but they are not letting us know!

Who were the first people to land **?**

The first men to set foot on the Moon's surface were Neil Armstrong and Buzz Aldrin on July 20th, 1969. It took them around four days to get there. They leaped around for two hours, collecting soil samples and taking photographs and, through satellite communications, even talked with US President Richard Nixon in the White House. It was then that Armstrong uttered the famous phrase, "One small step for man, one giant leap for mankind."

The image beams to thousands of TV sets.

FACT BYTES

An orange glass-like substance has been found on the Moon's surface, suggesting that there was once some volcanic activity.

The Moon does not have a "weather" system, so its rocks are not exposed to wind or water. Therefore, Buzz Aldrin's footprints are as fresh as when he made them!

A moon lander, the part of the spacecraft that descends onto the surface.

How much fuel do rockets need

The first stage engine of *Saturn V* gulped down fourteen tons of fuel every second while accelerating the spacecraft from 0-5,200 mph in 150 seconds. After eleven minutes, all three stages had been used and the rocket was traveling at 17,400 mph in orbit (that's nearly 5 miles traveled in every second).

What were the *Apollo* landings

Between 1969 and 1972, *Apollo* spacecraft landed on the Moon six times. An attempt by *Apollo 13* failed to land as there was an onboard explosion, but the spacecraft did manage to return to Earth safely. Each mission lasted around twelve days and astronauts visited different places each time. Astronomers gave these spots different names, like the "Sea of Tranquility" (a smooth area of ancient lava) and "Hadley Rille"—a V-shaped gorge, meandering among large mountains. The astronauts on *Apollo 15* traveled seventeen miles in a Land Roving Vehicle (LRV), an electrically powered four-wheel drive.

Why were the landings so important

We learned that the lunar craters were formed by asteroid impacts and not by volcanoes, and that the Moon almost certainly used to be a part of Earth. We confirmed that the Moon is slowly moving an inch or so away from Earth every year. We proved that human beings could live and work in space and would not suffer any ill effects. A huge amount of other information was collected, but it would take hundreds of books to describe it all!

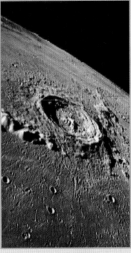

Lunar craters.

Part of Earth?

RETURN TO EARTH

Once the astronauts have gathered all the evidence that they need, taking samples from a landing or images from space, they need to return to Earth. (This could be after a considerable period—Russian Valeri Polyakov spent 438 long days in the *Mir* Space Station in 1994-95.) This needs very careful planning to ensure that the craft descends safely as it pushes through the Earth's atmosphere. Read on to find out how they do it.

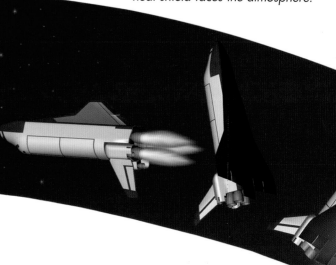

Retro-rockets fire to slow the Shuttle down and the spacecraft turns so the heat shield faces the atmosphere.

How does re-entry happen ?

Returning to Earth from orbit involves slowing the spacecraft down from a speed of nearly 5 miles per second to standstill. It would use up huge amounts of fuel to gradually slow a spacecraft down, so the trick is to enter Earth's atmosphere at just the right angle to slow you down safely. This involves some input from "space station" control on Earth and some direct contact from the commander.

Why is re-entry difficult ?

If the craft enters at too shallow an angle, it will bounce off the atmosphere. If it enters at too steep an angle, it will burn up and hit the ground at great speed. At the correct angle, the spacecraft heat shield or heat tiles will heat up to "only" 3,600-5,400°F and then the craft can land on a runway or use parachutes for safety.

A deck in a spacecraft.

A space station's controls.

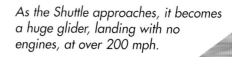

As the Shuttle approaches, it becomes a huge glider, landing with no engines, at over 200 mph.

As the Shuttle has no reverse thrust jet engines, a parachute and wheel brakes finally bring it to a stop.

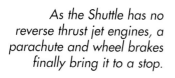

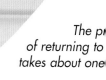

The pr of returning to takes about one

What happened to the Space Shuttle Columbia **?**

he Shuttle usually starts to ter the atmosphere on the dark side of the planet.

On February 1st, 2003, the Space Shuttle *Columbia* burned up on re-entry, killing all seven astronauts. It seems likely that a large chunk of insulation foam, which fell off the fuel tank at liftoff, damaged the Shuttle's heat-resistant tiles, causing the spacecraft to overheat on re-entry. In 1986, seven Shuttle astronauts were killed in the Shuttle *Challenger* due to a fault in the solid rocket boosters.

The Space Shuttle Columbia *blasts off.*

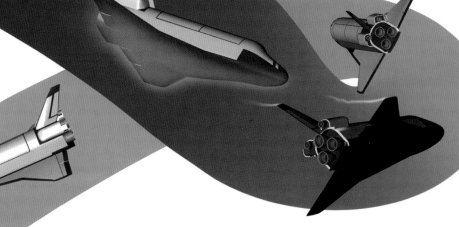

Below 1,000 mph, the Shuttle starts to land like a normal aircraft, weaving in S-shaped curves to further reduce speed.

The Shuttle enters the densest parts of the atmosphere at about 40,000 feet above Earth.

FACT BYTES

Some shuttles touch down onto a runway, in a similar way to a plane. They have a lifting body design and swept-back wings. When an orbiter "touches down" this way, the descent rate is SEVEN times steeper than that of an airliner!

Why can space shuttles use heat-resistant tiles **?**

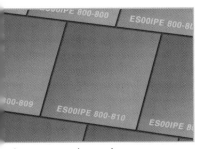

The ceramic heat tiles are reusable, but take a real bashing when they enter the atmosphere.

NASA space shuttles are designed to be reusable spacecraft that can be used on many missions. When they re-enter Earth's atmosphere, many of the heat-resistant tiles are damaged and need to be replaced. It is far easier to replace small tiles than replace one huge heat shield. The tiles are made of a special material that can be red hot on one side but stay cool on the other.

SATELLITES

Sending rockets into space and putting people on the Moon is highly exciting, but very expensive. In order to find out more about Earth and Earth's atmosphere, countries send "satellites" into space. These are highly complex objects equipped with an imaging and communication facility (to send images back to Earth) and enough propellant to boost them into orbit, and to stay there. Satellites still aren't cheap, though!

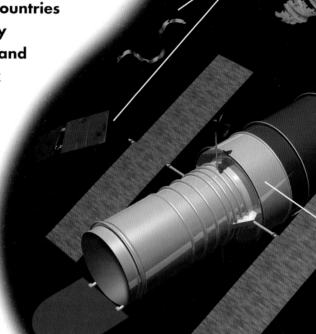

"Space junk" from broken u...

How high are the satellites ❓

Many scientific satellites are only 185-250 miles above Earth and orbit in under two hours. They are easy to launch, because the further out you place a satellite, the more fuel you need to put it there. Major communications satellites are put at a huge distance of 22,000 miles from Earth, because at that distance an orbit takes exactly one day to complete.

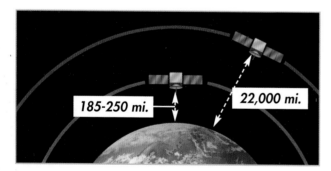

185-250 mi.　22,000 mi.

How many man-made satellites are out there ❓

Since the late 1950s, thousands of satellites and spacecraft have been launched around Earth, and over 10,000 objects now exist in orbit. Many of the early satellites have fallen back to Earth and burned up in the atmosphere, but there are thousands of items of "space-junk" in earth orbit and hundreds of relatively modern satellites.

What does a satellite do ❓

The working satellites orbiting Earth are of various types. There are telephone, TV and radio communications satellites, military spy satellites, weather satellites, and satellites studying the Sun and distant objects in the universe. There is also the Hubble space telescope, which is one of the largest objects orbiting Earth. The biggest object is the International Space Station.

We use satellites to communicate.

Some are used by the military.

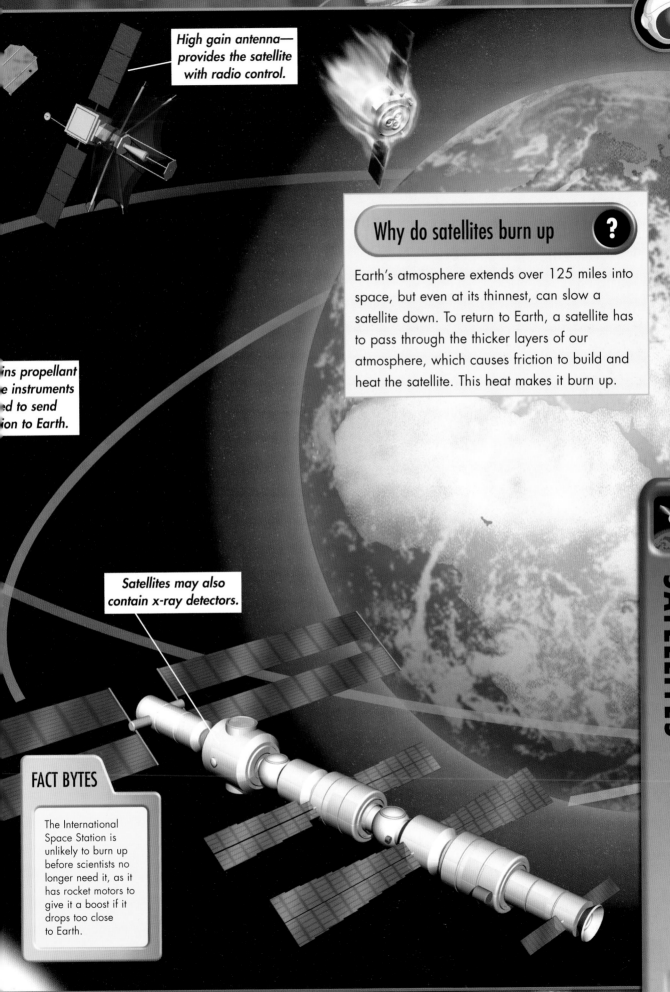

High gain antenna—provides the satellite with radio control.

...ins propellant ...e instruments ...d to send ...ion to Earth.

Why do satellites burn up ?

Earth's atmosphere extends over 125 miles into space, but even at its thinnest, can slow a satellite down. To return to Earth, a satellite has to pass through the thicker layers of our atmosphere, which causes friction to build and heat the satellite. This heat makes it burn up.

Satellites may also contain x-ray detectors.

FACT BYTES

The International Space Station is unlikely to burn up before scientists no longer need it, as it has rocket motors to give it a boost if it drops too close to Earth.

FUTURE MISSIONS

So what does the future hold? In the last century, humans have achieved things astronomers such as William Herschel could only dream of, with satellite images and Moon missions. If we are ever to send manned missions to the faraway planets of our Solar System, some major new technologies need to be developed— and there are some large challenges that need to be overcome.

Should we use humans or robots ?

At the moment, small robotic explorers appear to be the most efficient way of exploring space. The advances in computing power in recent years mean that very powerful and lightweight robot explorers can land on planets like Mars and trundle around the surface. Human beings are heavy and they need lots of food, water, and oxygen wherever they go. Humans also get homesick!

The *Mars Rover Explorer.*

The biggest advantage of using machines is that if robot explorers get destroyed it is just an expensive accident, but human beings cannot be replaced.

Will humans ever visit Mars ?

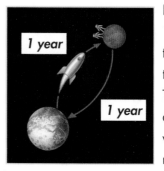

1 year

1 year

No-one knows. In the 1970s, NASA was talking about a mission to Mars in the 1980s! The problem is that if anything goes wrong on such a mission, there could be no rescue plan. A mission to Mars and back would probably take two years to complete and, in that time, members of the crew might become ill or unforeseen problems might develop. The other big problem is the cost. It could take a trillion dollars ($1,000,000,000,000) to send people to Mars.

How can we travel to distant planets more quickly ?

One of the most likely methods of powering our spacecraft to try to visit distant planets is to use nuclear power. Nuclear rockets are much more powerful than our existing chemically-fired launchers, and rockets run by nuclear fission are fuel efficient and very light. They could reach Saturn in three years instead of seven. The technology could be with us in around ten years. However, the use of this type of fuel is highly controversial. The rockets could release nuclear waste into the atmosphere, unless they used traditional methods for launching and then nuclear fuel when they were clear of the atmosphere.

FACT BYTES

Over 3,551,645 people just like you, had their names burned onto an electronic disk, attached to the Red Rover lander that is due to trawl the surface of Mars.

What else is coming up ?

The *Cassini-Huygens* spacecraft is due to orbit Saturn, only 12,500 miles above the cloud tops, and the lander is to descend onto Titan's surface, which could be an ocean of liquid methane!

Where will we go next ?

Most astronomers would like to think that at some point mankind will spread out into the Universe and explore other worlds, a bit like they do in *Star Trek*. However, there is one big problem: we don't have any really fast spaceships, so it takes months or years even to get to the closest planets in our Solar System. Rockets move forward by controlled explosions and not much has changed in the last 40 years. We need someone to invent a new propulsion system or to invent some form of anti-gravity!

next generation of space exploration needs faster spaceships.

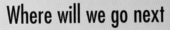

GLOSSARY

Aphelion
The furthest point from the Sun in a planet's orbit.

Astronaut
A person trained for traveling in space.

Astrophysics
The branch of astronomy that makes sense of numbers!

Atmosphere
The layer of gas surrounding Earth or other planets.

Aurora
The bright lights that atoms give off in the atmosphere at the North Pole. Also known as the "northern lights."

Big bang
A cataclysmic explosion that scientists believe created time and space.

Big crunch
What might happen if the universe stops expanding and collapses on itself.

Billion
A thousand million (1,000,000,000).

Black hole
A region of space caused by the collapse of a star, so dense that neither matter or radiation can escape.

Cassini division
The gap in Saturn's rings, discovered by astronomer G.D. Cassini.

Cassiopeia
An easily-spotted W-shaped constellation near the Pole star.

Centrifugal force
An imaginary force that helps us to imagine how things are "held together" on a rotating or curved path.

Comet
Pieces of ice and dust which orbit the Sun.

Constellation
Any of the 88 groups of stars as seen from Earth, named by the Greeks after mythological people, objects or animals.

Convective zone
The "layer" of the sun which receives heat from the radiative zone.

As this zone is more dense (less gassy), the heat is able to rise and make its way out into the atmosphere.

Corona
The very hot outer layer of the Sun's atmosphere.

Cosmonaut
A Russian trained for space travel.

Ellipse
A shape like a flattened circle.

Equator
The name for the imaginary band around the middle of Earth that splits it into two hemispheres, the north and the south.

Evening Star
Another common name for Venus.

Fission
The splitting of the centers of heavy atoms into lighter ones.

Fusion
The combining of lighter elements into heavier ones.

Galaxy
A collection of billions of stars held together by gravitational attraction.

Great Red Spot
A long-lived feature on Jupiter's surface, south of its equator, which has survived for 200–300 years.

Hemispheres
The two halves of the globe, as divided by an imaginary line around the middle called the equator.

Hydrosphere
The water on, or around, the surface of a planet.

International Space Station
A satellite constructed between 1998 and 2001 for space research.

Kelvin
A temperature scale in which the lowest possible temperature is called "absolute zero."

Lunar-Roving Vehicle
An electronically powered four-wheel drive vehicle.

Light year
The distance that light travels in one year. It is equal to just under 6 trillion miles!

LINEAR
Also NEAT—Telescopes which discover asteroids and comets.

Lithosphere
The crust of a planet.

Lunar eclipse
When Earth passes between the Sun and the Moon.

Magellanic clouds
Small, irregular galaxies near the Southern Celestial Pole.

Magnetosphere
A magnetic field around the Sun and certain planets.

Magnitude scale
The scale on which objects are measured for their brightness.

Mariner
A series of American space probes which visited Mercury, Venus, and Mars.

Messier
A catalogue named after an eighteenth century astronomer which identifies galaxies and nebulae etc. by their number i.e. M31 (Andromeda Galaxy).

Meteor
A very small iron or rocky particle that has entered Earth's atmosphere. Also called a shooting star.

Milky Way
A blurred band of light stretching across the night sky including millions of faint stars.

Miranda
One of Uranus' largest moons, with a unique surface.

Nova
When a binary star undergoes an eruption and suddenly becomes much brighter.

Observatory
A building specially designed to look at astrological objects.

Olympus Mons
A massive volcano on the surface of Mars.

Orbit
The path a planet takes when encircling the Sun.

Photosphere
The area of the Sun that we look at, face-on.

Radiative zone
The heat from the Sun's core is passed through to this zone, and the energy transfer begins. It then reaches the less dense area of the convective zone where it rises and starts to reach the atmosphere.

Rings
Any of the thin, circular bands made from small components that orbit something larger i.e. Saturn.

Sea of Tranquility
A smooth area of ancient lava on the surface of the Moon—made famous by the *Apollo 11* landing.

Solar eclipse
When the Moon comes between the Sun and Earth.

Solar flare
A sudden brightening near a sunspot.

Solar System
The system containing the Sun and other bodies in its gravitational field, including the Moon and nine known planets.

Sunspot
A dark blemish on the solar surface that is caused by the Sun's magnetic field.

Sunspot cycle
The eleven-year cycle that sees the rise and fall in the number of sunspots.

Supernova
When a star runs out of fuel, it becomes unstable and appears 100 million times brighter for a few days before "dying."

White dwarf
A small, very dense star that has come to the end of its life.

GLOSSARY

INDEX

Key: Top - t; middle - m; bottom - b; left - l; right -r

Front and back cover: Stephen Sweet, Photodisc and Corel.

2: (bl) NASA. **5:** (tr) Topham Picturepoint. **22:** Science Photo Library. **32:** (t, bl) NASA. **33:** (t, br) NASA. **34:** NASA. **35:** (tr) 2002 ESA - ARIANESPACE/ Photo Service Otique CSG. **37:** (tr, br) NASA. **38:** (t) Corel. **39:** (bm) NASA. **41:** (tr) NASA. **44:** (ml) NASA. **48:** NASA.

Illustrations by Stephen Sweet/SGA.